KS2 MATHS
SATs SUCCESS
10–MINUTE TESTS

Ages 9–10

KS2 MATHS SATs

10–MINUTE TESTS

PAUL BROADBENT

Sample page

clear instructional text

topic being covered

test number for quick reference

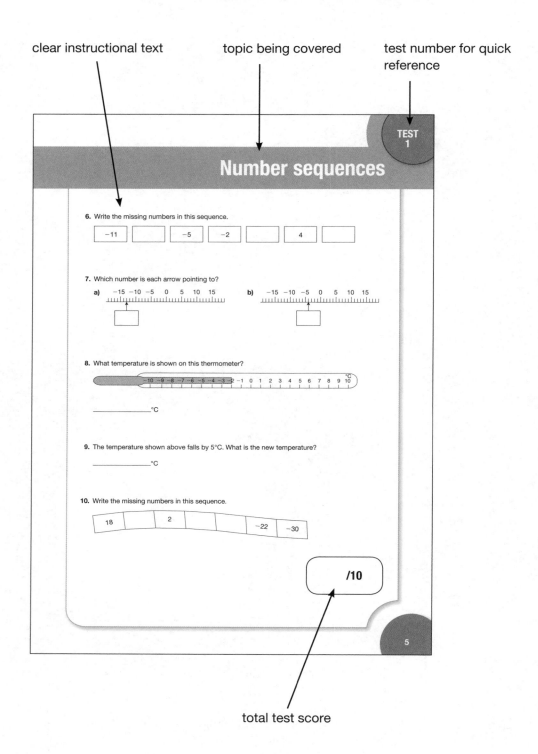

TEST 1

Number sequences

6. Write the missing numbers in this sequence.

| −11 | | −5 | −2 | | 4 | |

7. Which number is each arrow pointing to?

a) −15 −10 −5 0 5 10 15

b) −15 −10 −5 0 5 10 15

8. What temperature is shown on this thermometer?

−10 −9 −8 −7 −6 −5 −4 −3 −2 −1 0 1 2 3 4 5 6 7 8 9 10 °C

_____ °C

9. The temperature shown above falls by 5°C. What is the new temperature?

_____ °C

10. Write the missing numbers in this sequence.

| 18 | | 2 | | | −22 | −30 |

/10

5

total test score

Contents

Number sequences

 1. Write the next three numbers in this sequence.

| 63 | 74 | 85 | 96 | 107 | 118 | 129 |

 2. Write the missing numbers in this sequence.

| 14 | 8 | 2 | −4 | −10 | −16 | 22 |

 3. Which number is each arrow pointing to?

a) −15 −10 −5 0 5 10 15

−2

b) −15 −10 −5 0 5 10 15

−11

 4. What temperature is shown on this thermometer?

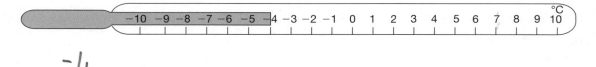

_____−4_____ °C

 5. The temperature shown above rises by 6°C. What is the new temperature?

_____2_____ °C

Number sequences

6. Write the missing numbers in this sequence.

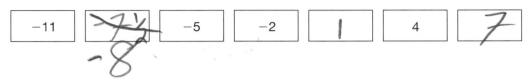

| −11 | ~~−7~~ −8 | −5 | −2 | 1 | 4 | 7 |

7. Which number is each arrow pointing to?

a)   −15 −10 −5   0   5   10   15

−13

b)   −15 −10 −5   0   5   10   15

−4

8. What temperature is shown on this thermometer?

°C
−10 −9 −8 −7 −6 −5 −4 −3 −2 −1 0 1 2 3 4 5 6 7 8 9 10

__−2__ °C

9. The temperature shown above falls by 5°C. What is the new temperature?

__−7 B__ °C

10. Write the missing numbers in this sequence.

| 18 | 10 | 2 | −8 −14 | −22 | −30 |

8 **/10**

Decimals

1. Draw lines to match the decimals to the fractions.

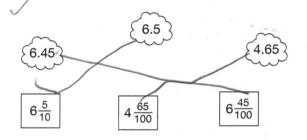

6.45   6.5   4.65

$6\frac{5}{10}$ $4\frac{65}{100}$ $6\frac{45}{100}$

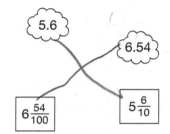

5.6   6.54

$6\frac{54}{100}$ $5\frac{6}{10}$

2. Write the decimals indicated by the arrows on this number line.

6   7   8

6.1   6.5   7.2   7.9 ✗

3. Write these fractions as decimals.

a) $\frac{34}{100}$ → 0.34

b) $\frac{19}{100}$ → 0.19

c) $\frac{7}{100}$ → 0.07

4. Change these decimals to hundredths.

a) 0.51 → $\frac{51}{100}$

b) 0.92 → $\frac{92}{100}$

c) 0.08 → $\frac{8}{100}$

5. Rearrange each of these to make a decimal number as close to 4 as possible.

a) ⑧ ③
   ④ ⋅

   348 †

b) ⑤ ①
   ⋅ ②

   5.12

c) ⑨ ④
   ② ⋅

   249

   4.99

6. Write the missing decimals indicated by arrows on this number line.

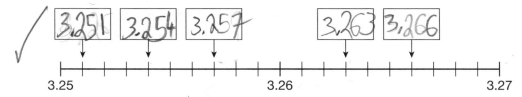

3.251 3.254 3.257   3.263 3.266

3.25   3.26   3.27

7. Write the value of the circled digits as tenths or hundredths.

a) 8.⑨25 → $\frac{9}{10}$ b) 13. 11⑧ → $\frac{8}{1000}$ c) 10. 0⑤5 → $\frac{50}{100}$

8. Write these as decimals.

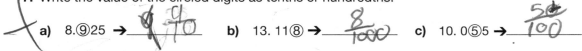

0.021

a) $\frac{1}{1000}$ → 0.001   b) $\frac{21}{1000}$ → 0.01   c) $\frac{900}{1000}$ → 0.9

9. Write this as a decimal number.

$400 + 80 + 6 + \frac{700}{100} + \frac{900}{1000} + \frac{5}{1000}$ = $\frac{1605}{1000}$ 0.605 486.605 ?

(486) $\frac{1605}{1000}$

10. Change these decimals to whole numbers and thousandths.

a) 6.249 → $6\frac{249}{1000}$ b) 3.021 → $3\frac{21}{1000}$ c) 7.555 → $7\frac{555}{1000}$

$\frac{1}{10} = 0.1$ $\frac{1}{1000}$ 0.01 $\frac{1}{1000}$ 0.001

7 **/10**

7

Ordering numbers

1. Write the sign < or > for each pair of numbers.

a) 20 056 ___<___ 20 506

b) 39 989 ___>___ 39 898

2. Circle the largest number in each pair.

a) (745.5)   745.09

b) (36.85)   36.58

c) 1207.14   (1270.03)

3. Write these numbers in order, starting with the smallest.

(29 945)   (208 865)   (29 906)   (208 956)   (290 030)

29906 29945 208865 208956 290030

4. Tick the smallest amount in this set.

35.78 kg ☐   30.19 kg ☑   35.8 kg ☐   30.3 kg ☐   30.47 kg ☐

5. Write <, > or = between each pair of decimals.

a) 0.011 ___<___ 0.111   b) 0.42 ___>___ 0.402   c) 0.658 ___>___ 0.568

6. These temperatures should be in order, starting with the lowest temperature.
Colour the two temperatures that have been swapped.

−10°C   −1°C   −4°C   −7°C   2°C   5°C

7. Write these lengths in order, starting with the shortest.

| 37.45 m | 38.33 m | 37.91 m | 38.3 m | 37.5 m |

37.45m 37.5m 37.91m 38.3m 38.33m

8. These are the costs of five train tickets. Write the prices in order, starting with the most expensive.

£38.70

£31.29

£74.88

£40.05

£60.90

£74.88 £60.90 £40.05 £38.70 £31.29

9. Write the number that is halfway between each pair.

a)   5000   10 000

7500

b)   0   50 000

25000

10. Write these temperatures in order, starting with the lowest.

−17°C   3°C   0°C   −19°C   −11°C   −20°C

−20°C −19°C −17°C −11°C 0°C 3°C

10 **/10**

Rounding and approximating

1. Draw lines to join these numbers to the nearest 10.

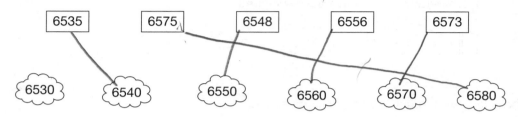

| 6535 | | 6575 | | 6548 | | 6556 | | 6573 |

6530   6540   6550   6560   6570   6580

2. Round these numbers to the nearest 1000.

a) 16 869 → _17,000_   b) 28 055 → _28000_   c) 49 344 → _49000_

3. Round these numbers to the nearest pound.

a) £18.48 → _£18_   b) £27.52 → _£28_   c) £49.61 → _£50_

4. Write two decimal numbers that would round to 12 as the nearest whole number.

_12.4_ and _11.9_

5. Round each of these to the nearest 100 g.

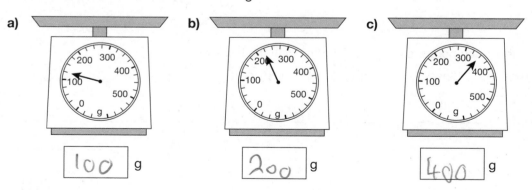

a) _100_ g   b) _200_ g   c) _400_ g

Rounding and approximating

6. Estimate how much liquid is in this jug in millilitres.

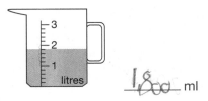

_____1800_____ ml

7. Circle the number that is nearest to the correct answer for each of these.

a)   144 + 262 =   350   (400)   450

b)   352 − 147 =   (200)   250   300

8. Round each number in these calculations to the nearest 10 to give an approximate answer.

a)   1438 + 327 ➜ _1770_   b)   1902 − 578 ➜ _1320_

9. Draw lines to join these decimals to the nearest whole number.

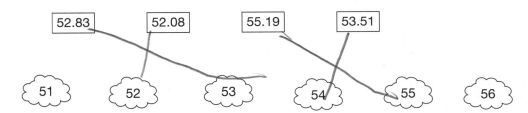

| 52.83 | 52.08 | | 55.19 | 53.51 |

51   52   53   54   55   56

10. Approximately how many hours are there in February in a leap year? Circle the correct range.

100–200 hours   (300–400 hours)   (600–700 hours)   800–900 hours

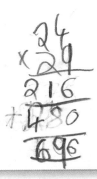

$$\begin{array}{r} 24 \\ \times\,24 \\ \hline 216 \\ +\,480 \\ \hline 696 \end{array}$$

9 /10

Fractions, decimals and percentages

1. Write these as improper fractions.

a)

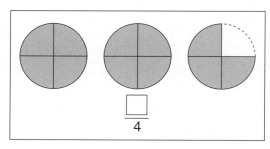

$\dfrac{\square}{4}$

b)

$\dfrac{\square}{3}$

2. Change these improper fractions to whole numbers and fractions.

a) $\dfrac{9}{2}$ = _____

b) $\dfrac{15}{4}$ = _____

c) $\dfrac{18}{5}$ = _____

d) $\dfrac{20}{3}$ = _____

3. Complete this table to show the matching fractions, decimals and percentages.

Fractions	Decimals	Percentages
$\dfrac{1}{2}$		50%
	0.2	
		75%
$\dfrac{3}{10}$		

4. Write the percentage of the grid that is shaded.

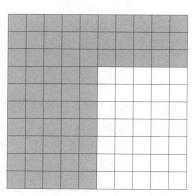

_____%

5. Write these fractions as percentages.

a) $\dfrac{35}{100}$ = _____

b) $\dfrac{1}{4}$ = _____

c) $\dfrac{40}{50}$ = _____

Fractions, decimals and percentages

6. Colour these scales to show each percentage.

a)

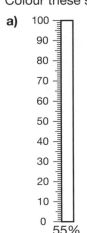

55%

b)

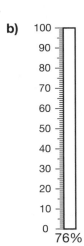

76%

7. Draw lines to join the matching fractions, decimals and percentages.

$\frac{1}{5}$	$\frac{3}{10}$	$\frac{45}{100}$	$\frac{4}{5}$
0.3	0.2	0.8	0.45
80%	45%	30%	20%

8. Write these percentages as fractions.

a) 90% = ▭

b) 5% = ▭

c) 60% = ▭

9. Use > or < to complete these.

a) 0.8 _____ 8%

b) 0.2 _____ 50%

c) 0.25 _____ 75%

10. Change these to improper fractions.

a) $4\frac{3}{4}$ → ▭

b) $2\frac{1}{2}$ → ▭

c) $5\frac{2}{3}$ → ▭

/10

Equivalent fractions

1. Write each fraction indicated by the matching shaded areas, in two ways.

a)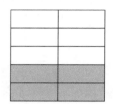

$$\frac{\boxed{}}{\boxed{}} = \frac{\boxed{}}{\boxed{}}$$

b)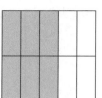

$$\frac{\boxed{}}{\boxed{}} = \frac{\boxed{}}{\boxed{}}$$

2. Cross out the fraction that is not equivalent.

a)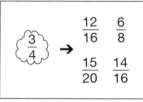

$$\frac{3}{4} \rightarrow \quad \frac{12}{16} \quad \frac{6}{8}$$
$$\frac{15}{20} \quad \frac{14}{16}$$

b)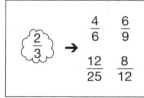

$$\frac{2}{3} \rightarrow \quad \frac{4}{6} \quad \frac{6}{9}$$
$$\frac{12}{25} \quad \frac{8}{12}$$

3. Complete this equivalent fraction chain.

$$\frac{2}{5} = \frac{4}{\boxed{}} = \frac{\boxed{}}{15} = \frac{8}{\boxed{}} = \frac{\boxed{}}{25}$$

4. Write the fraction shaded, using the smallest possible denominator.

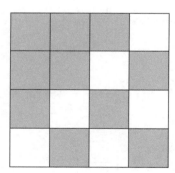

_____

5. Complete these equivalent fractions.

a) $\frac{3}{10} = \frac{\boxed{}}{50}$

b) $\frac{5}{6} = \frac{15}{\boxed{}}$

c) $\frac{2}{3} = \frac{40}{\boxed{}}$

Equivalent fractions

6. Shade $\frac{2}{3}$ of this circle.

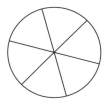

7. Write down the fraction shaded on this shape. Then work out the equivalent fraction with the smallest possible denominator.

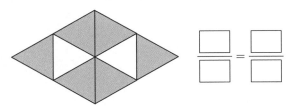

8. Complete this equivalent fraction chain.

$$\frac{5}{8} = \frac{\Box}{16} = \frac{15}{\Box} = \frac{\Box}{32} = \frac{25}{\Box}$$

9. Simplify each fraction so that you have the smallest possible denominator.

a) $\frac{6}{15} = \frac{\Box}{\Box}$

b) $\frac{25}{100} = \frac{\Box}{\Box}$

c) $\frac{14}{16} = \frac{\Box}{\Box}$

10. Write four different fractions that are equivalent to $\frac{3}{5}$.

/10

Ratio and proportion

Colour these tile patterns to match the ratios.

1. The ratio of red to blue is one to every three.

2. The ratio of green to yellow is one to every four.

3. The ratio of black to white is three to every five.

4. In a cake recipe, 25 g of cherries are needed for every 100 g of raisins. What weight of cherries is needed for a cake that has 800 g of raisins?

_____ g

5. What proportion of this grid is shaded? Give your answer as a fraction, using the smallest possible denominator.

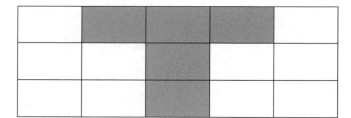

Ratio and proportion

6. In a group of 20 children, 12 are girls and 8 are boys. What proportion of the group are girls? Write your answer as a fraction, using the smallest possible denominator.

7. This is a recipe for six people. Write out the ingredients needed for just two people.

Fish Pie (for six people)	Fish Pie (for two people)
600 g fish	_____ g fish
1.5 kg potatoes	_____ g potatoes
300 g peas	_____ g peas
240 g cheese	_____ g cheese
120 g butter	_____ g butter
180 ml milk	_____ ml milk

8. What is the ratio of grey to white tiles? Give the ratio in its simplest form.

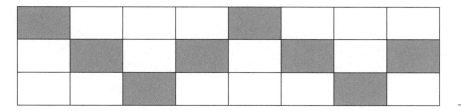

_____

9. In a book of 40 pages, two out of every five of the pages have a picture on them. How many pages have a picture?

_____

10. 12 red beads and 16 white beads are kept in a bag. What is the ratio of red to white beads? Give the ratio in its simplest form.

_____

/10

Multiplication and division facts

1. Write the missing numbers.

   a) $7 \times$ _____ $= 56$

   b) _____ $\times 9 = 54$

   c) $4 \times$ _____ $= 32$

2. Complete these multiplication grids.

a)

×	7	9	6
8			
7			
4			

b)

×	10	11	12
8			
9			
10			

3. Answer these.

   a) $27 \div 3 =$ _____

   b) $42 \div 6 =$ _____

   c) $56 \div 7 =$ _____

4. Which two numbers less than 50 can be divided exactly by 2, 3, 4, 6, 8 and 12?

   _____   _____

5. Draw lines to join each division to its matching remainder.

25 ÷ 3	44 ÷ 5	68 ÷ 9	51 ÷ 8	44 ÷ 6

 1   2   3   4   5

Multiplication and division facts

6. Write two different multiplications for each answer. Do not use the number 1 and, in each answer, you must use four different numbers.

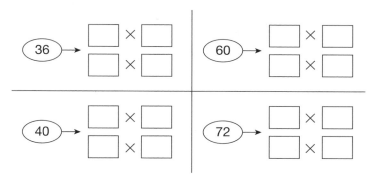

7. Complete these multiplication grids.

a)

×	9		6
3			
8		40	
			42

b)

×	7	4	
8			64
		36	
			24

8. Write the missing numbers.

a) $30 \times$ _____ $= 180$

b) _____ $\times 4 = 200$

c) $50 \times$ _____ $= 350$

9. I am thinking of a number. If I divide it by 6 and then add 2, the answer is 7. What number am I thinking of?

_____

10. I am thinking of a number. If I multiply it by 8 and then subtract 2, the answer is 30. What number am I thinking of?

_____

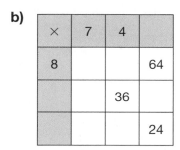

/10

Factors and multiples

1. Write the factors of these numbers in order.

a) 32 → | 1, 2, |

b) 20 → | |

c) 25 → | |

d) 55 → | |

2. Answer these.

a) The 5th multiple of 4 is… _____.

b) The 6th multiple of 3 is… _____.

c) The 4th multiple of 9 is… _____.

3. Write the three smallest numbers that will fit into the central shaded part of each Venn diagram.

a)

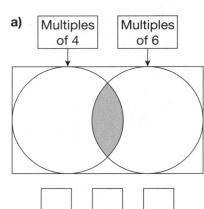

Multiples of 4   Multiples of 6

☐ ☐ ☐

b)

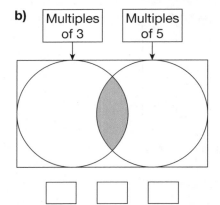

Multiples of 3   Multiples of 5

☐ ☐ ☐

4. Write the factors of these numbers in pairs.

a) 28 → (1, 28) _____

b) 45 → _____

c) 40 → _____

d) 24 → _____

5. 3 is a factor of 123. Tick the correct answer.

True ☐   False ☐

Factors and multiples

Use this set of numbers to answer questions 6–8.

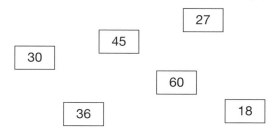

6. Which three numbers are multiples of both 3 and 5?

_____   _____   _____

7. Which two numbers are multiples of 9, but not multiples of 6?

_____   _____

8. Which number is a multiple of 2, 3, 4, 5, 6 and 10?

_____

9. Circle the correct answer.

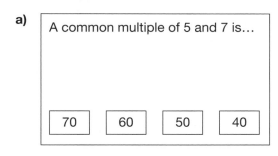

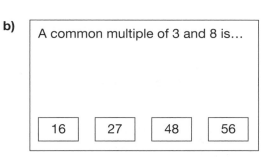

a) A common multiple of 5 and 7 is…

| 70 | 60 | 50 | 40 |

b) A common multiple of 3 and 8 is…

| 16 | 27 | 48 | 56 |

10. 17 is a prime number. Tick the correct answer.

True ☐   False ☐

How do you know?

/10

Addition

1. Answer these.

    a) 108 + 53 = _____

    b) 125 + 91 = _____

    c) 146 + 72 = _____

2. Four pairs of these numbers each total 5000. Write the pairs.

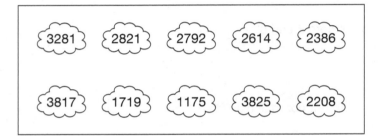

_____ and _____   _____ and _____

_____ and _____   _____ and _____

3. Answer these.

  a)   4 1 4 7   **b)**   3 2 0 9   **c)**   5 2 3 8   **d)**   6 3 6 4

      + 2 1 6 4   + 1 1 5 8   + 4 1 8 5   + 5 2 7 7

      _____   _____   _____   _____

4. What is the perimeter of this shape?

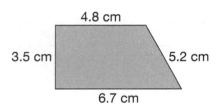

_____ cm

Addition

5. Add each row and column to find the total in the bottom right-hand corner.

7.2	9.1	
6.4	8.9	

6. Answer these.

a)
```
   1 4 1 0 5
+  3 2 6 3 9
_____

```

b)
```
   2 7 6 8 2
+  4 1 5 0 8
_____

```

c)
```
   5 3 8 5 7
+  2 4 7 9 4
_____

```

7. Sam goes shopping and spends £37.45 on a pair of trainers and £18.99 on a tracksuit. How much does he spend in total?

£_____

8. Write the missing digits.

a)
```
  [ ] 3  1  5
+   1  5 [ ] 2
_____
    9  8  7  7
```

b)
```
    4  8  2  9
+   3 [ ] 5 [ ]
_____
    7  9  8  1
```

c)
```
    4 [ ] 2  9
+   2  7 [ ] 3
_____
    7  0  2  2
```

9. Draw lines to join pairs of numbers that total £30.

£18.75   £11.25   £10.25   £15.85

£12.55   £19.75   £14.15   £17.45

10. Write the missing digits.

| 3 | | 9 | + | 7 | | = | 4 | 2 | 5 |

/10

Subtraction

1. Draw lines to join pairs with a difference of 88.

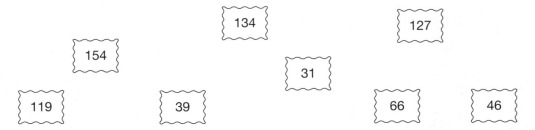

2. Answer these.

a)
```
  3 0 2 9
− 1 3 6 2
─────────
```

b)
```
  5 6 1 4
− 2 7 9 5
─────────
```

c)
```
  7 2 0 4
− 4 9 1 6
─────────
```

3. Write the change from £10 for each of these.

a) £3.58

b) £8.27

c) £6.09

4. Write the missing digits.

a)
```
  3 8 1
− 1 □ 9
───────
  2 3 □
```

b)
```
  4 □ 8
− □ 9 3
───────
  1 8 5
```

c)
```
  6 0 4
− 3 □ 5
───────
  □ 2 □
```

5. I am thinking of a number. If I subtract 255 from it, the answer is 89.
What number am I thinking of?

_____

Subtraction

This diagram shows the distances by road of some cities from London in kilometres.

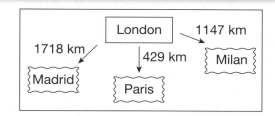

6. How much further is it from London to Madrid than from London to Paris?

_____ km

7. How much further is it from London to Madrid than from London to Milan?

_____ km

8. Answer these.

a)   6 3 2 1 5
     − 2 0 9 4 3
     _____

b)   4 0 3 8 7
     − 1 9 4 7 9
     _____

c)   8 3 0 1 6
     − 5 6 1 7 8
     _____

9. Write the difference between each pair.

a)

_____ litres

b)
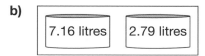

_____ litres

10. A plank of wood is 2.14 metres in length. It is cut into two pieces. If one of the pieces is 0.79 metres, what is the length of the other piece?

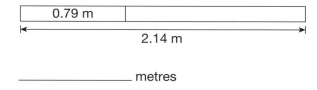

_____ metres

/10

Multiplication

1. Double each of these numbers.

a) 316 → ◻

b) 185 → ◻

c) 259 → ◻

2. This is a ×80 machine. Complete the table.

 IN → ×80 → OUT

IN	6		3		9
OUT		560		400	

3. Tick the multiplication that has the largest product.

| 78 × 4 ◻ | 57 × 6 ◻ | 94 × 3 ◻ | 48 × 7 ◻ |

4. Answer these. Show your method in the boxes below.

a) 159 × 6 = ◻

b) 374 × 8 = ◻

5. A magazine costs £3.48 per month. What is the cost for six months' subscription to the magazine?

£ _____

£3.48

Multiplication

6. Answer these. Show your method in the boxes below.

a) $38 \times 49 =$ ☐

b) $57 \times 26 =$ ☐

7. What is the area of each of these rectangles?

a)

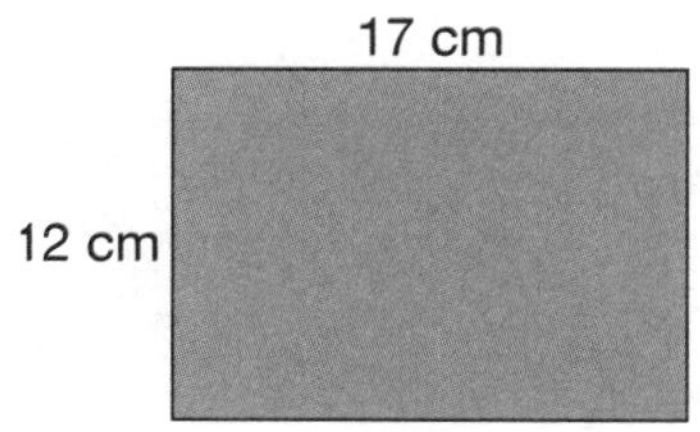

17 cm

12 cm

Area = ☐ cm²

b)

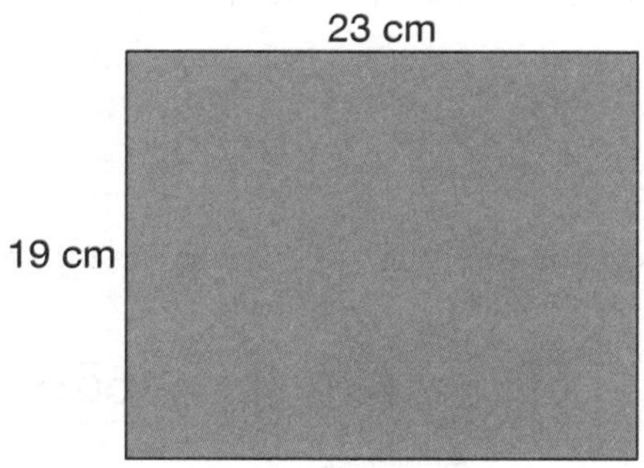

23 cm

19 cm

Area = ☐ cm²

8. A box weighs 28 kg. What is the weight of 15 boxes?

_____ kg

9. Answer these.

a)
```
  1 3 7 4
×       8
─────────
```

b)
```
  3 2 0 9
×       6
─────────
```

c)
```
  5 4 7 8
×       4
─────────
```

10. What is the product of 425 and 19?

_____

/10

Division

1. Answer these. Show your method in the boxes below.

   a) 67 ÷ 4 = [ ]

   b) 106 ÷ 3 = [ ]

2. Write the missing numbers in each of these.

   a) _____ ÷ 8 = 15

   b) _____ ÷ 3 = 19

3. This is a ÷**100** machine. Complete the table.

   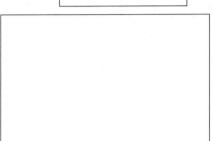

IN	490		245		705
OUT		3.7		6.81	

4. Answer these.

   a) 6)384

   b) 5)295

   c) 7)791

5. Tick the numbers that are not exactly divisible by 3.

143	219	171	206	316	378
☐	☐	☐	☐	☐	☐

Division

6. A tube holds six tennis balls. How many tubes are needed for each of these quantities of tennis balls? Some of the tubes may not be full.

a) 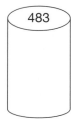 483

b) 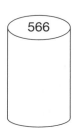 566

c) 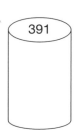 391

d) 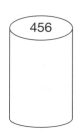 456

_____   _____   _____   _____

7. Answer these.

a) 4)5375

b) 5)2836

c) 3)1509

8. Write the missing digits to complete these.

a) ☐ 4 9 r ☐
   5)7 4 9

b)   3 5 r ☐
   8)☐ 8 5

c)   5 9 r ☐
   9)5 ☐ 7

9. Which number between 90 and 100 has a remainder of 1 when it is divided by 8?

_____

10. What is the smallest number you can add to 490 to make it exactly divisible by 4?

_____

/10

Fractions and percentages

1. Answer each of these.

a)

$\frac{3}{5}$ of...

25 → _____
40 → _____
50 → _____
65 → _____

b)

$\frac{2}{3}$ of...

24 → _____
30 → _____
42 → _____
90 → _____

2. Answer these.

a) 10% of £2 = _____

b) 25% of £20 = _____

c) 20% of £10 = _____

3. In a maths test, Emma scored 18 out of 20. The following week she scored 45 out of 50 in a different test. What were the percentage scores for each test?

a) $\frac{18}{20}$ = _____ %

b) $\frac{45}{50}$ = _____ %

4. What fraction of the grid is left white? Write it in its simplest form.

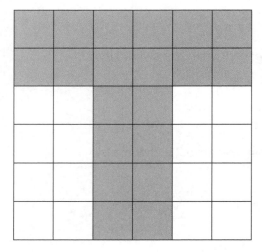

_____

5. What is $\frac{3}{4}$ of each of these?

a) 52 kg

_____ kg

b) 600 ml

_____ ml

c) 900 g

_____ g

d) 120 cm

_____ cm

Fractions and percentages

6. These are the ingredients for an 800 g cake. Write the weight of each ingredient.

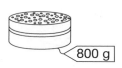

800 g

Recipe
30% flour
20% butter
10% sugar
25% raisins
10% cherries
5% walnuts

Ingredients	
flour	_____ g
butter	_____ g
sugar	_____ g
raisins	_____ g
cherries	_____ g
walnuts	_____ g

7. Answer these.

a) 10% of £75 = ☐

b) 20% of £75 = ☐

c) 5% of £75 = ☐

d) 15% of £75 = ☐

8. A bag contains 60 marbles. $\frac{1}{3}$ of them are red, $\frac{2}{5}$ of them are blue and $\frac{1}{10}$ of them are yellow. The rest of the marbles are green. What fraction of the marbles in the bag are green?

_____

9. Circle the largest amount.

$\frac{5}{8}$ of 56 litres $\frac{4}{7}$ of 63 litres

10. What is 5% of each of these?

a) 80 kg → _____ kg

b) 30 kg → _____ kg

c) 140 kg → _____ kg

/10

Number puzzles

Write the missing numbers on each of these grids.

1.

5	+	3	=	
+		−		−
	+		=	
=		=		=
	−	3	=	5

2.

4	+	4	=	
+		×		−
	+		=	7
=		=		=
9	−		=	

3.

	+	6	=	
×		÷		−
3	×		=	
=		=		=
12	÷		=	4

4.

	÷		=	2
−		÷		×
	−	2	=	
=		=		=
4	×		=	12

5.

24	÷	6	=	
÷		×		×
	÷	2	=	
=		=		=
	×		=	24

6.

6	×		=	36
×		÷		÷
	×		=	6
=		=		=
	×		=	6

Arithmogons

In each of these, the number in the box is the total of the two numbers in the circles on either side. Write the missing numbers.

1. (3) —□— (8)

2.

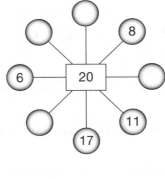

3.

4.

5.

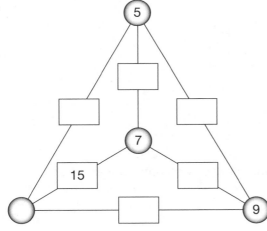

6.

2-D shapes

1. Draw lines to match each name to the correct regular shape.

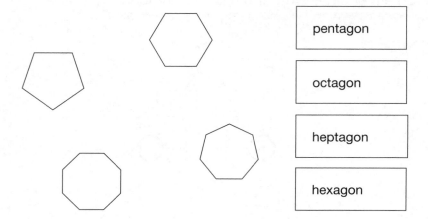

pentagon

octagon

heptagon

hexagon

2. Complete the table for these triangles.

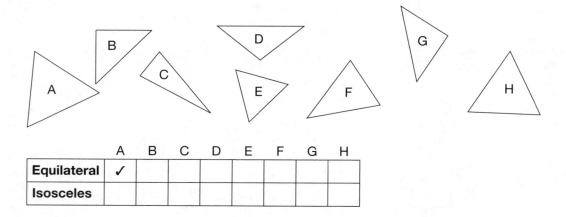

	A	B	C	D	E	F	G	H
Equilateral	✓							
Isosceles								

3. Which of the triangles above have a right angle? _____

4. An isosceles triangle has a line of symmetry. Is this always, sometimes or never true?

_____

5. What is the name of this shape?

   _____

2-D shapes

6. Draw lines to join each triangle to the correct place on the Venn diagram.

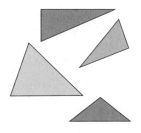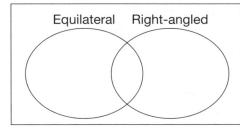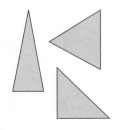

Equilateral   Right-angled

7. Draw a quadrilateral on this grid which has opposite sides of equal length but no right angles.

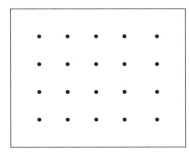

8. A quadrilateral is symmetrical. Is this always, sometimes or never true?

_____

9. Tick each shape that has parallel sides.

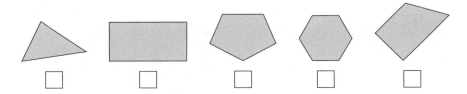

☐   ☐   ☐   ☐   ☐

10. Draw a line perpendicular to AB from C.

A   C   B

/10

3-D shapes

1. Complete the table for these 3-D shapes.

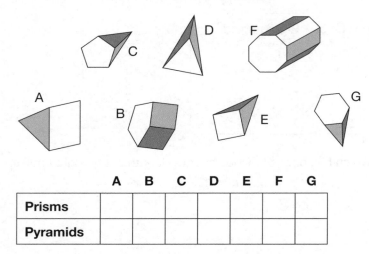

	A	B	C	D	E	F	G
Prisms							
Pyramids							

2. How many faces, edges and vertices does a cube have?

_____ faces

_____ edges

_____ vertices

3. Name the shapes made from each net.

a)

b)

_____   _____

4. A pyramid has four faces. Is this always, sometimes or never true?

_____

5. How many vertices does a triangular prism have?

_____

6. Tick the tetrahedron in this set of pyramids.

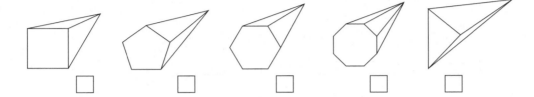

☐   ☐   ☐   ☐   ☐

7. How many edges does a tetrahedron have? _____

8. Name the shapes made from each net.

a)
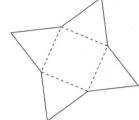

b)
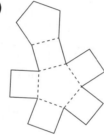

_____   _____

9. Name this 3-D shape.

 _____

10. Draw a prism and a pyramid starting from a triangle.

a)

prism

b)

pyramid

/10

Position and direction

Write the position on the grid of each shape.

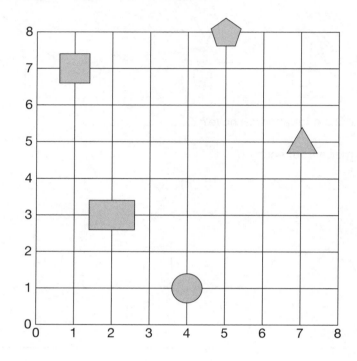

1. rectangle → _____

2. pentagon → _____

3. square → _____

4. triangle → _____

5. circle → _____

Position and direction

Each of these grids has a mirror line. Draw the reflection of each shape on the grid.

6.

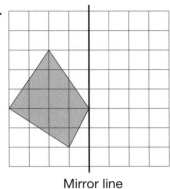

Mirror line

7.

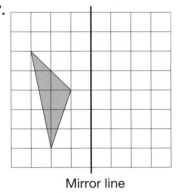

Mirror line

8.

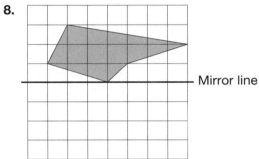

Mirror line

9.

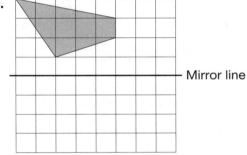

Mirror line

10. This grid has two mirror lines.

Draw the reflection of the shape.

Mirror line

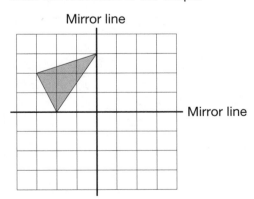

Mirror line

/10

Roman numerals

1. Write these as numbers:

   a) XI _____   b) XIX _____   c) XXI _____

2. Write these as Roman numerals:

   a) 17 _____   b) 24 _____   c) 29 _____

3. Write the missing Roman numerals on this clock:

4. Write < or > to make these true:

   a) XXXII _____ XXIV   b) LXIII _____ LXX

5. XC is 90 in Roman numerals. Tick the correct answer.

   True ☐   False ☐

   Explain how you know.

6. Write these in order, starting with the smallest:

LIV   LX   XLV   L   LVIII

_____

7. a) Write the missing numeral in this sequence:

DXXX   DXXXI   DXXXII   DXXXIII   _____   DXXXV   DXXXVI   DXXXVII

b) Write the missing Roman numeral as a number: _____

8.

The digits 6, 3 and 5 can make these numbers:

563 ⟶ DLXIII

653 ⟶ DCLIII

Make two more numbers from these three digits and write them as Roman numerals:

a) _____ ⟶ _____

b) _____ ⟶ _____

9. Circle the largest number:

DCCXVII   DCCXXIV

10. What year is shown by MMXV? _____

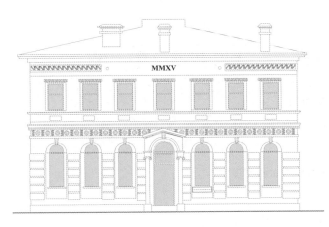

/10

Angles

1. Tick all the acute angles in these shapes.

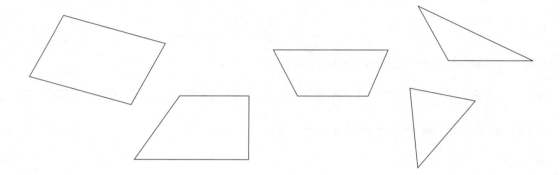

2. Draw an obtuse angle on this grid.

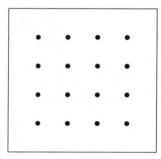

3. Estimate these angles. For each of the two angles, circle the angle in the box that is nearest your estimate.

a)

| 30° | 40° | 50° | 60° |

b)

| 110° | 130° | 150° | 170° |

4. What is the interior angle sum of a rectangle?

_____

5. True or false? An obtuse angle is between 90° and 180°.

_____

Angles

6. Use a protractor or angle measurer to measure this angle.

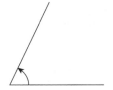

7. What is the interior angle sum of an equilateral triangle? _____

8. How many degrees are there in three right angles? _____

9. Write the size of the missing angles on these straight lines. Do not measure the angles.

a)

? 120°

b)

? 45°

c)

? 100°

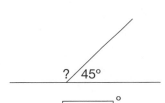

10. Write the size of the missing angles in these right angles. Do not measure the angles.

a)

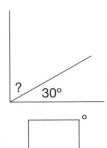

? 30°

b)

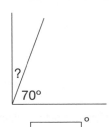

? 70°

c)

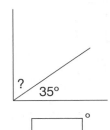

? 35°

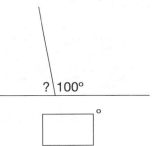

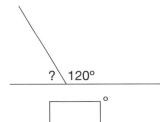

/10

Standard units of measure

1. Write these lengths.

    a)   4.2 m   = _____ cm   **b)**   6.3 km   = _____ m

    c)   78 mm   = _____ cm   **d)**   80 cm   = _____ m

> Underline the amount each item is most likely to measure.

2. My bedroom is (3.8 cm) (3.8 m) (30.8 m) (3.8 km) across from one wall to the other.

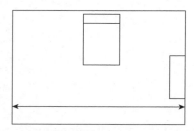

3. A loaf of bread weighs (85 g) (850 g) (8.5 kg) (8.5 g).

4. I put my (2.2 ml) (22 l) (22 ml) (2.2 l) carton of orange juice in the fridge.

5. Measure the length of this line in centimetres and in millimetres.

[   ] cm = [   ] mm

Standard units of measure

6. What is 850 m less than 6 km?

_____ km or _____ m

7. Complete these.

    a)   6.7 kg = _____ g

    b)   3.95 kg = _____ g

    c)   8200 g = _____ kg

    d)   4750 g = _____ kg

8. What is the difference in length between these two lines?

Difference = _____ mm

9. What must be added to each amount to make 5 kg?

    a)

    1450 g + [ ] g

    b)

    2850 g + [ ] g

10. Complete these.

    a)   5.9 litres = _____ ml

    b)   8.65 litres = _____ ml

    c)   3400 ml = _____ litres

    d)   7250 ml = _____ litres

/10

Reading scales

1. What is the reading on each of these scales?

a)

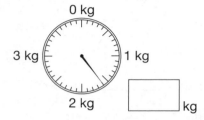

□ kg

b)

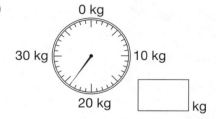

□ kg

2. Write each reading in millimetres.

a)

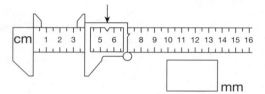

□ mm

b)

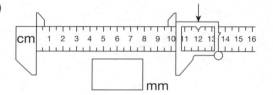

□ mm

3. How much liquid is in each jug? Write the amounts in millilitres.

a)

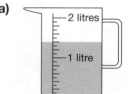

_____ ml

b)

_____ ml

4. Write these lengths in millimetres.

□ mm   □ mm

cm 1 2 3 4 5 6 7 8 9 10 11 12 13 14 15

5. What is the difference in length between the arrows in question 4?

Difference = □ mm

6. 110 ml of liquid is added to this container. How much liquid will there be in total?

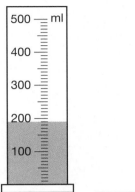

_____ ml

7. What is the reading on each of these scales?

a)

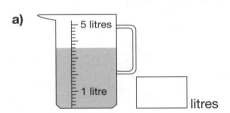

☐ kg

b)

20 kg

10 kg | 30 kg

0 kg

☐ kg

8. What is the difference between the two readings in question 7? _____ kg

9. How much liquid is in each jug? Write the amounts in litres.

a)

5 litres

1 litre

☐ litres

b)

5 litres

1 litre

☐ litres

10. 400 g of flour is taken off these scales.
What will the new reading be?

☐ kg

/10

Perimeter

1. Draw a rectangle on this grid with a perimeter of 30 squares.

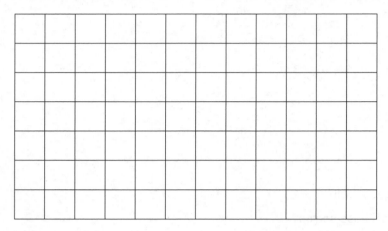

2. A square has sides of 35 mm each. What is the perimeter of the square?

_____ mm

3. What is the perimeter of this rectangle?

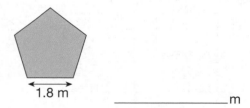

_____ m

4. What is the perimeter of a regular pentagon with sides of 1.8 metres each?

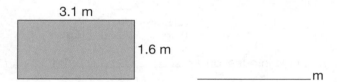

_____ m

5. What is the perimeter of this shape?

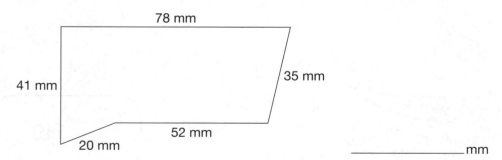

_____ mm

6. Draw two different shapes on this grid, each with a perimeter of 14 cm.

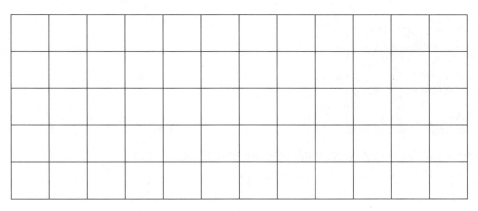

7. What is the perimeter of a square with an area of 81 cm²?

_____ cm

8. A rectangle has a perimeter of 64 mm. If the length of each of the longest sides is 21 mm, what is the length of each of the shortest sides?

_____ mm

9. What is the perimeter of this shape?

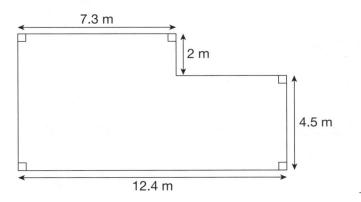

_____ m

10. What is the perimeter of an equilateral triangle in which each side measures 8.3 cm? Write your answer in millimetres.

_____ mm

/10

Area

1. What is the area of this rectangle?

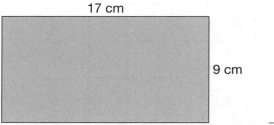

17 cm

9 cm

_____ cm²

2. Draw two different shapes on this grid, each with an area of 14 squares.

3. A square has a perimeter of 48 cm. What is the area of the square?

Perimeter = 48 cm

Area = ☐ cm²

4. A rectangle has an area of 96 cm². If one of the longer sides is 16 cm, what is the length of the shorter sides?

_____ cm

5. What is the area of this room?

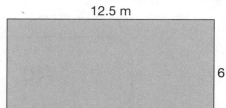

12.5 m

6 m

_____ m²

6. Draw a rectangle on this grid with an area of 24 cm².

7. A square has an area of 49 cm².
What is the perimeter of the square?

Area = 49 cm²

Perimeter = _____ cm

8. This shape has two parts, A and B. What is the area of each part?

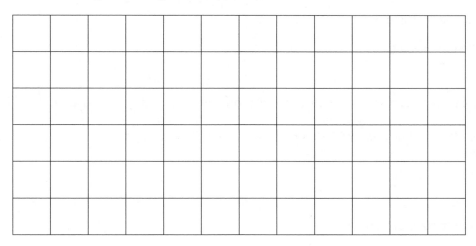

a) Area of A = _____ cm²

b) Area of B = _____ cm²

9. What is the total area of the shape, A + B, in question 8?

Total area = _____ cm²

10. A rectangle has an area of 120 cm². If one of the longer sides is 15 cm, what is the length of the shorter sides?

_____ cm

/10

Time

1. Write these as 24-hour clock times.

    a)   8 o'clock in the morning ➔ _____

    b)   8 o'clock in the evening ➔ _____

2. A train starts its journey at 13:50 and completes the journey 2 hours 30 minutes later.

    What time does the journey end? Write your answer as a 24-hour clock time.

    _____

3. Write these as 24-hour clock times.

    a)   a.m.

    | : |

    b)   a.m.

    | : |

    c)   p.m.

    | : |

4. Complete these.

    a)   1800 seconds = _____ minutes

    b) $10\frac{1}{2}$ minutes = _____ seconds

    c) $8\frac{1}{2}$ hours = _____ minutes

    d)   720 hours = _____ days

5. If the time is 11.38 a.m., what time will it be in $3\frac{1}{2}$ hours? Write your answer using a.m. or p.m.

    _____

6. Draw hands on the clocks to show these times.

a)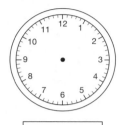

10 : 42

b)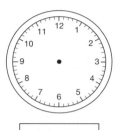

14 : 08

c)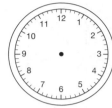

20 : 36

7. If today is Thursday 1ˢᵗ May, what date was it yesterday?

_____

8. Write these 24-hour clock times using a.m. or p.m.

a) 16:45 → _____

b) 11:53 → _____

c) 23:05 → _____

9. A train takes 1 hour 15 minutes between each stop. Complete the timetable.

Aston	10:42		
Bunstone		15:25	
Caleby	13:12		20:44

10. Write these times using the 24-hour clock.

a) 10.35 p.m. → _____

b) 8.49 a.m. → _____

c) 3.55 p.m. → _____

/10

Fraction calculations

1. What is the total of these two fractions?

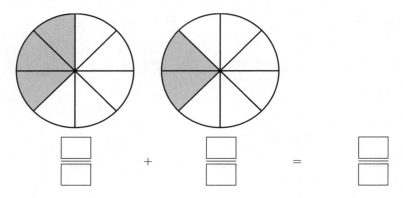

$$\boxed{} \atop \boxed{} \quad + \quad \boxed{} \atop \boxed{} \quad = \quad \boxed{} \atop \boxed{}$$

2. What is the difference between these two fractions?

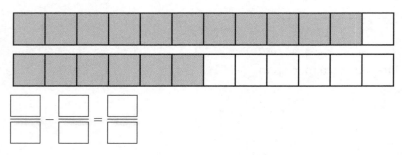

$$\frac{\boxed{}}{\boxed{}} - \frac{\boxed{}}{\boxed{}} = \frac{\boxed{}}{\boxed{}}$$

3. Colour the rectangle to show this addition.

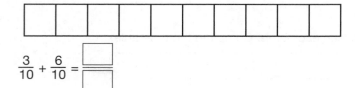

$$\frac{3}{10} + \frac{6}{10} = \frac{\boxed{}}{\boxed{}}$$

4. $\frac{1}{2}$ of this bar of chocolate is eaten by Sam and then a further $\frac{1}{4}$ is broken off and eaten by Amy. How many squares of chocolate are left?

_____

Fraction calculations

5. Write the totals of these fractions in their simplest form.

a) $\dfrac{3}{5} + \dfrac{1}{5} = \dfrac{\square}{\square}$ **b)** $\dfrac{3}{10} + \dfrac{2}{10} = \dfrac{\square}{\square}$ **c)** $\dfrac{1}{2} + \dfrac{1}{4} = \dfrac{\square}{\square}$

6. Colour the rectangle to show this addition.

$\dfrac{3}{4} + \dfrac{1}{8} = \dfrac{\square}{\square}$

7. a) Answer this:

$\dfrac{7}{10} - \dfrac{3}{5} = \dfrac{\square}{\square}$

b) Shade these rectangles to show the first two fractions of the sum in 7a.

8. Circle the missing fraction:

$\dfrac{\square}{\square} + \dfrac{5}{6} = 1\dfrac{1}{6}$

$\dfrac{1}{6}$ $\dfrac{5}{6}$ $\dfrac{1}{2}$ $\dfrac{1}{3}$ $\dfrac{2}{3}$

9. A pizza is cut into 12 equal slices. Emma eats $\dfrac{1}{3}$ of it and Ali eats $\dfrac{1}{6}$ of it. How many slices are left?

_____

/10

10. Answer these, giving your answers in the simplest form:

a) $\dfrac{7}{10} - \dfrac{3}{10} = \dfrac{\square}{\square}$ **b)** $\dfrac{11}{12} - \dfrac{7}{12} = \dfrac{\square}{\square}$ **c)** $\dfrac{1}{2} - \dfrac{1}{4} = \dfrac{\square}{\square}$

Tables, charts and graphs

This bar chart shows the maths test scores of a group of children. Use the information in the bar chart to answer the questions.

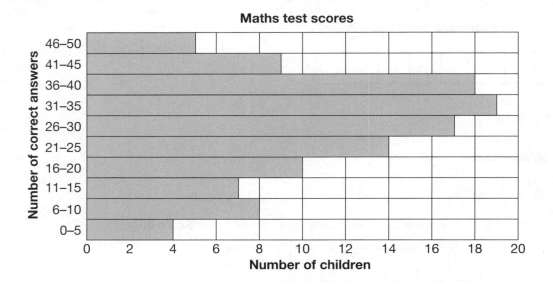

Maths test scores

1. How many children scored between 26 and 30 correct answers?

   _____

2. How many children scored between 46 and 50 correct answers?

   _____

3. How many children altogether scored more than 30 correct answers?

   _____

4. How many children altogether scored 20 or fewer correct answers?

   _____

5. What was the **mode** range of scores for this maths test?

   _____

Tables, charts and graphs

This graph shows the performance of a cyclist in a race.

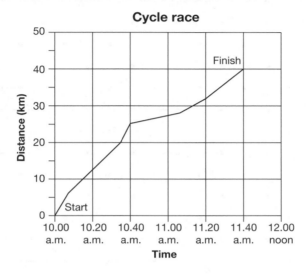

Cycle race

6. What time did the race start?

_____

7. How far had the cyclist travelled after 1 hour?

_____

8. At what time had the cyclist travelled 32 kilometres?

_____

9. What was the length of the race?

_____

10. How long did it take for the cyclist to complete the race?

_____

/10

Shape puzzle

Add one extra triangle to each shape to make it symmetrical.
Colour each shape to make symmetrical patterns.

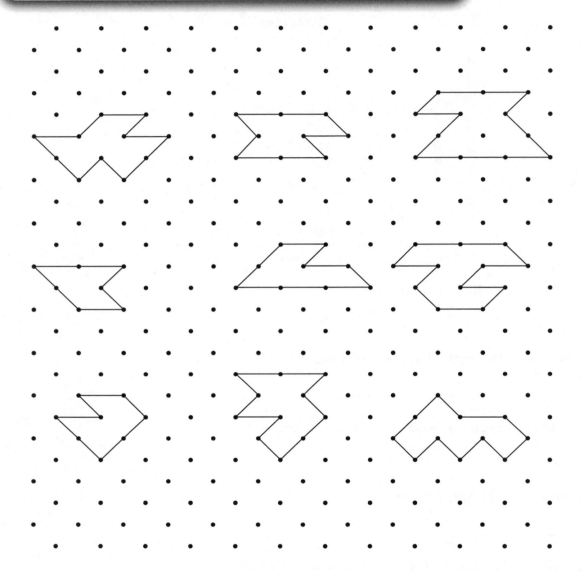

Maths maze

Move horizontally or vertically one number at a time through this maze to the finish. You can only move on to a number that is a multiple or factor of the number you are on.

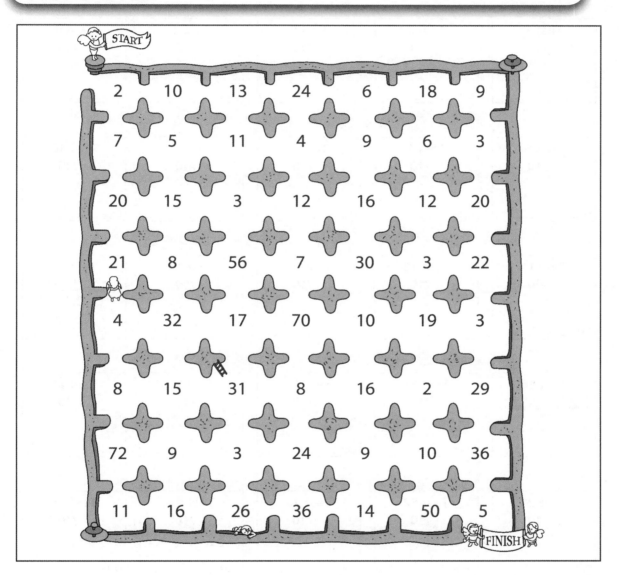

Progress report

Record how many questions you got right and the date you completed each test.
This will help you to monitor your progress.

Test 1 /10	Test 2 /10	Test 3 /10	Test 4 /10	Test 5 /10
Date _____	Date _____	Date _____	Date _____	Date _____

Test 6 /10	Test 7 /10	Test 8 /10	Test 9 /10	Test 10 /10
Date _____	Date _____	Date _____	Date _____	Date _____

Test 11 /10	Test 12 /10	Test 13 /10	Test 14 /10	Test 15 — If you got all of the missing numbers in less than 10 minutes, score yourself 10 marks.
Date _____	Date _____	Date _____	Date _____	Date _____

Test 16 — If you did this in less than 10 minutes, score yourself 10 marks.	Test 17 /10	Test 18 /10	Test 19 /10	Test 20 /10
Date _____	Date _____	Date _____	Date _____	Date _____

Test 21 /10	Test 22 /10	Test 23 /10	Test 24 /10	Test 25 /10
Date _____	Date _____	Date _____	Date _____	Date _____

Test 26 /10	Test 27 /10	Test 28 /10	Test 29 — If you complete all the shapes, score yourself 10 marks.	Test 30 — If you complete the maze, score yourself 10 marks.
Date _____	Date _____	Date _____	Date _____	Date _____

Answers: Maths 10-Minute Tests, age 9–10

Test 1
1. 107   118   129
2. 8   −16   −22
3. a) −2   b) −11
4. −4°C
5. 2°C
6. −8   1   7
7. a) −13   b) −4
8. −2°C
9. −7°C
10. 10   −6   −14

Test 2
1. 6.45 → $6\frac{45}{100}$
   6.5 → $6\frac{5}{10}$
   4.65 → $4\frac{65}{100}$
   5.6 → $5\frac{6}{10}$
   6.54 → $6\frac{54}{100}$
2. 6.1   6.5   7.2   7.8
3. a) 0.34   b) 0.19   c) 0.07
4. a) $\frac{51}{100}$ b) $\frac{92}{100}$ c) $\frac{8}{100}$
5. a) 3.84   b) 5.12   c) 4.29
6. 3.251 3.254 3.257 3.263 3.266
7. a) 9 tenths
   b) 8 thousandths
   c) 5 hundredths
8. a) 0.001   b) 0.021   c) 0.9
9. 486.795
10. a) $6\frac{249}{1000}$ b) $3\frac{21}{1000}$ c) $7\frac{555}{1000}$

Test 3
1. a) 20 056 < 20 506
   b) 39 989 > 39 898
2. a) 745.5   b) 36.85
   c) 1270.03
3. 29 906   29 945   208 865
   208 956   290 030
4. 30.19 kg
5. a) 0.011 < 0.111
   b) 0.42 > 0.402
   c) 0.658 > 0.568
6. −7°C   −1°C
7. 37.45 m   37.5 m   37.91 m
   38.3 m   38.33 m
8. £74.88   £60.90   £40.05
   £38.70   £31.29
9. a) 7500   b) 25 000
10. −20°C   −19°C   −17°C
    −11°C   0°C   3°C

Test 4
1. 6535 → 6540
   6575 → 6580
   6548 → 6550
   6556 → 6560
   6573 → 6570
2. a) 17 000
   b) 28 000
   c) 49 000
3. a) £18
   b) £28
   c) £50

4. Any two numbers from
   11.5 to 12.49
5. a) 100 g   b) 200 g   c) 400 g
6. 1800 ml
7. a) 400   b) 200
8. a) 1770   b) 1320
9. 52.83 → 53
   52.08 → 52
   55.19 → 55
   53.51 → 54
10. 600–700 hours (696 hours)

Test 5
1. a) $\frac{11}{4}$ b) $\frac{4}{3}$
2. a) $4\frac{1}{2}$ b) $3\frac{3}{4}$
   c) $3\frac{3}{5}$ d) $6\frac{2}{3}$
3.

Fractions	Decimals	Percentages
$\frac{1}{2}$	0.5	50%
$\frac{1}{5}$	0.2	20%
$\frac{3}{4}$	0.75	75%
$\frac{3}{10}$	0.3	30%

4. 65%
5. a) 35%   b) 25%   c) 80%
6.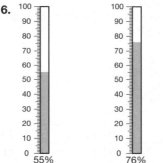
   55%   76%
7. $\frac{1}{5}$ → 0.2 → 20%
   $\frac{3}{10}$ → 0.3 → 30%
   $\frac{45}{100}$ → 0.45 → 45%
   $\frac{4}{5}$ → 0.8 → 80%
8. a) $\frac{90}{100}$ or $\frac{9}{10}$
   b) $\frac{5}{100}$ or $\frac{1}{20}$
   c) $\frac{60}{100}$ or $\frac{3}{5}$ or $\frac{6}{10}$
9. a) 0.8 > 8%   b) 0.2 < 50%
   c) 0.25 < 75%
10. a) $\frac{19}{4}$ b) $\frac{5}{2}$ c) $\frac{17}{3}$

Test 6
1. a) $\frac{4}{10} = \frac{2}{5}$ b) $\frac{3}{5} = \frac{6}{10}$
2. a) $\frac{14}{16}$ b) $\frac{12}{25}$
3. $\frac{2}{5} = \frac{4}{10} = \frac{6}{15} = \frac{8}{20} = \frac{10}{25}$
4. $\frac{5}{8}$
5. a) $\frac{3}{10} = \frac{15}{50}$ b) $\frac{5}{6} = \frac{15}{18}$
   c) $\frac{2}{3} = \frac{40}{60}$

6.
7. $\frac{6}{8} = \frac{3}{4}$
8. $\frac{5}{8} = \frac{10}{16} = \frac{15}{24} = \frac{20}{32} = \frac{25}{40}$
9. a) $\frac{2}{5}$ b) $\frac{1}{4}$ c) $\frac{7}{8}$
10. Check that the fractions are
    equivalent to $\frac{3}{5}$,
    e.g. $\frac{6}{10}, \frac{9}{15}, \frac{12}{20}, \frac{15}{25}$

Test 7
1. 3 red and 9 blue tiles
2. 3 green and 12 yellow tiles
3. 6 black and 10 white tiles
4. 200 g
5. $\frac{1}{3}$
6. $\frac{3}{5}$
7. 200 g fish
   500 g potatoes
   100 g peas
   80 g cheese
   40 g butter
   60 ml milk
8. 1 to 2 or 1:2
9. 16
10. 3 to 4 or 3:4

Test 8
1. a) 8   b) 6   c) 8
2. a)

×	7	9	6
8	56	72	48
7	49	63	42
4	28	36	24

b)

×	10	11	12
8	80	88	96
9	90	99	108
10	100	110	120

3. a) 9   b) 7   c) 8
4. 24 and 48
5. 25 ÷ 3 → r1
   44 ÷ 5 → r4
   68 ÷ 9 → r5
   51 ÷ 8 → r3
   44 ÷ 6 → r2
6. 36 → Any two from 2 × 18,
        3 × 12, 4 × 9
   60 → Any two from 2 × 30,
        3 × 20, 4 × 15, 5 × 12,
        6 × 10
   40 → Any two from 2 × 20,
        4 × 10, 5 × 8
   72 → Any two from 2 × 36,
        3 × 24, 4 × 18, 6 × 12,
        8 × 9

7. a)

×	9	5	6
3	**27**	**15**	18
8	**72**	40	**48**
7	**63**	**35**	42

b)

×	7	4	8
8	**56**	**32**	64
9	**63**	36	**72**
3	**21**	**12**	24

8. a) 6   **b)** 50   **c)** 7

9. 30

10. 4

Test 9

1. a) 1, 2, 4, 8, 16, 32
   b) 1, 2, 4, 5, 10, 20
   c) 1, 5, 25
   d) 1, 5, 11, 55

2. a) 20.
   b) 18.
   c) 36.

3. a) 12, 24, 36   **b)** 15, 30, 45

4. a) (1, 28) (2, 14) (4, 7)
   b) (1, 45) (3, 15) (5, 9)
   c) (1, 40) (2, 20) (4, 10) (5, 8)
   d) (1, 24) (2, 12) (3, 8) (4, 6)

5. True

6. 30, 45, 60

7. 45, 27

8. 60

9. a) 70   **b)** 48

10. True. Because it has no factors
    except for 1 and itself.

Test 10

1. a) 161   **b)** 216   **c)** 218

2. 1175 and 3825
   3281 and 1719
   2386 and 2614
   2208 and 2792

3. a) 6311   **b)** 4367
   c) 9423   **d)** 11641

4. 20.2 cm

5.

7.2	9.1	**16.3**
6.4	8.9	**15.3**
13.6	**18**	**31.6**

6. a) 46744 **b)** 69190 **c)** 78651

7. £56.44

8. a) **8**315 + 15**6**2 = 9877
   b) 4829 + 3**15**2 = 7981
   c) 4**2**29 + 27**9**3 = 7022

9. £18.75 → £11.25
   £19.75 → £10.25
   £12.55 → £17.45
   £15.85 → £14.15

10. 349 + 7**6** = 425

Test 11

1. 154 → 66
   127 → 39
   134 → 46
   119 → 31

2. a) 1667   **b)** 2819   **c)** 2288

3. a) £6.42   **b)** £1.73   **c)** £3.91

4. a) 381 − 149 = 23**2**
   b) 478 − 2**9**3 = 185
   c) 604 − 375 = **2**29

5. 344

6. 1289 km

7. 571 km

8. a) 42272 **b)** 20908 **c)** 26838

9. a) 5.58 litres   **b)** 4.37 litres

10. 1.35 metres

Test 12

1. a) 632   **b)** 370   **c)** 518

2.

IN	6	7	3	5	9
OUT	**480**	560	**240**	400	**720**

3. 57 × 6 (= 342)

4. a) 954   **b)** 2992

5. £20.88

6. a) 1862   **b)** 1482

7. a) 204 cm²   **b)** 437 cm²

8. 420 kg

9. a) 10992 **b)** 19254 **c)** 21912

10. 8075

Test 13

1. a) 16 r 3
   b) 35 r 1

2. a) 120
   b) 57

3.

IN	490	**370**	245	**681**	705
OUT	**4.9**	3.7	**2.45**	6.81	**7.05**

4. a) 64   **b)** 59   **c)** 113

5. 143   206   316

6. a) 81 **b)** 95 **c)** 66 **d)** 76

7. a) 1343 r 3
   b) 576 r 1
   c) 503

8. a) 149 r **4**   **b)** 35 r **5**
     5) 749   8) 285

   c) 59 r **6**
      9) 537

9. 97

10. 2

Test 14

1. a) $\frac{3}{5}$ of…   **b)** $\frac{2}{3}$ of…

    25 → 15   24 → 16
    40 → 24   30 → 20
    50 → 30   42 → 28
    65 → 39   90 → 60

2. a) 20p   **b)** £5   **c)** £2

3. a) 90%   **b)** 90%

4. $\frac{4}{9}$

5. a) 39 kg   **b)** 450 ml
   c) 675 g   **d)** 90 cm

6. flour 240 g
   butter 160 g
   sugar 80 g
   raisins 200 g
   cherries 80 g
   walnuts 40 g

7. a) £7.50
   b) £15
   c) £3.75
   d) £11.25

8. $\frac{1}{6}$

9. $\frac{4}{7}$ of 63 litres

10. a) 4 kg   **b)** 1.5 kg   **c)** 7 kg

Test 15

1.

5	+	3	=	8
+		−		−
3	+	0	=	3
=		=		=
8	−	3	=	5

2.

4	+	4	=	8
+		×		−
5	+	2	=	7
=		=		=
9	−	8	=	1

3.

4	+	6	=	10
×		÷		−
3	×	2	=	6
=		=		=
12	÷	3	=	4

4.

12	÷	6	=	2
−		÷		×
8	−	2	=	6
=		=		=
4	×	3	=	12

5.

24	÷	6	=	4
÷		×		×
12	÷	2	=	6
=		=		=
2	×	12	=	24

6.

6	×	6	=	36
×		÷		÷
1	×	6	=	6
=		=		=
6	×	1	=	6

Test 16

1.
   (3) — [11] — (8)

2.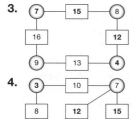
   (5)
   [11] [13]
   (6) [14] (8)

3.
   (7) [15] (8)
   [16]   [12]
   (9) [13] (4)

4.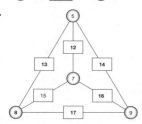
   (3) [10] (7)
   [8] [12] [15]
   (5) [13] (8)

5.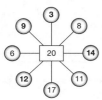
   (5)
   [12]
   [13]   [14]
   (7)
   [15]   [16]
   (8) [17] (9)

6.
   (9) (3) (8)
   (6) [20] (14)
   (12) (17) (11)

Test 17

1. ⬠ pentagon   ⬡ hexagon
   ⯃ octagon   ⯂ heptagon

2.

	A	B	C	D	E	F	G	H
Equilateral	✓				✓			✓
Isosceles		✓	✓	✓		✓	✓	

3. B and G
4. always true
5. rhombus
6.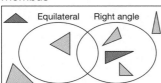
   Equilateral   Right angle

7. Check that a parallelogram or rhombus has been drawn.
8. sometimes true
9. 2nd, 4th and 5th shapes should be ticked.
10. A vertical line should be drawn from C (at right angles to line AB).

Test 18

1.

	A	B	C	D	E	F	G
Prisms	✓	✓				✓	
Pyramids			✓	✓	✓		✓

2. 6 faces, 12 edges and 8 vertices
3. a) triangular pyramid or tetrahedron
   b) triangular prism
4. sometimes true
5. 6
6. The 5th shape should be ticked.
7. 6
8. a) square-based pyramid
   b) pentagonal prism
9. cylinder
10. a) Check that a prism has been drawn.
    b) Check that a pyramid has been drawn.

Test 19

1. rectangle ➔ (2, 3)
2. pentagon ➔ (5, 8)
3. square ➔ (1, 7)
4. triangle ➔ (7, 5)
5. circle ➔ (4, 1)
6. 7.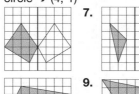
8. 9.
10.

Test 20

1. a) 11   b) 19   c) 21
2. a) XVII   b) XXIV   c) XXIX
3.
4. a) XXXII > XXIV   b) LXIII < LXX
5. True. Because X = 10 and C = 100. 100 − 10 = 90.
6. XLV   L   LIV   LVIII   LX
7. a) DXXXIV   b) 534
8. 365 ➔ CCCLXV;
   356 ➔ CCCLVI; 536 ➔ DXXXVI;
   635 ➔ DCXXXV
9. DCCXXIV
10. 2015

Test 21

1.

2. Check that an angle between 90° and 180° has been drawn.
3. a) 40°   b) 110°
4. 360°
5. true
6. 65°
7. 180°
8. 270°
9. a) 60°   b) 135°   c) 80°
10. a) 60°   b) 20°   c) 55°

Test 22

1. a) 420 cm
   b) 6300 m
   c) 7.8 cm
   d) 0.8 m
2. 3.8 m
3. 850 g
4. 2.2 l
5. 7.9 cm = 79 mm
6. 5.15 km or 5150 m
7. a) 6700 g
   b) 3950 g
   c) 8.2 kg
   d) 4.75 kg
8. 15 mm
9. a) 3550 g
   b) 2150 g
10. a) 5900 ml
    b) 8650 ml
    c) 3.4 litres
    d) 7.25 litres

Test 23

1. a) 1.6 kg   b) 24 kg
2. a) 55 mm   b) 120 mm
3. a) 1400 ml   b) 1900 ml
4. 25 mm   85 mm
5. 60 mm
6. 300 ml
7. a) 1.8 kg   b) 15 kg
8. 13.2 kg
9. a) 3.6 litres   b) 2.5 litres
10. 2.2 kg

Test 24

1. Check rectangle has a perimeter of 30 squares, e.g. 9 × 6.
2. 140 mm
3. 9.4 m
4. 9 m
5. 226 mm
6. Check both shapes have a perimeter of 14 cm.
7. 36 cm

8. 11 mm
9. 37.8 m
10. 249 mm

Test 25
1. 153 cm²
2. Check that the area of each shape is 14 squares.
3. 144 cm²
4. 6 cm
5. 75 m²
6. Check rectangle has an area of 24 cm², e.g. 12 cm × 2 cm, 8 cm × 3 cm, 6 cm × 4 cm.
7. 28 cm
8. a) 36 cm²
   b) 12 cm²
9. 48 cm²
10. 8 cm

Test 26
1. a) 08:00
   b) 20:00
2. 16:20
3. a) 08:55 b) 11:05 c) 14:25
4. a) 30 minutes
   b) 630 seconds
   c) 510 minutes
   d) 30 days
5. 3.08 p.m.
6. a)
   10 : 42

   b)
   14 : 08

c)
20 : 36

7. Wednesday 30th April
8. a) 4.45 p.m.
   b) 11.53 a.m.
   c) 11.05 p.m.
9.

Aston	10:42	**14:10**	**18:14**
Bunstone	**11:57**	15:25	**19:29**
Caleby	13:12	**16:40**	20:44

10. a) 22:35 b) 08:49 c) 15:55

Test 27
1. $\frac{3}{8} + \frac{2}{8} = \frac{5}{8}$
2. $\frac{11}{12} - \frac{6}{12} = \frac{5}{12}$
3. $\frac{9}{10}$

4. 4
5. a) $\frac{4}{5}$ b) $\frac{1}{2}$ c) $\frac{3}{4}$
6.

$\frac{7}{8}$
7. a) $\frac{1}{10}$
   b)

8. $\frac{1}{3}$
9. 6 slices
10. a) $\frac{2}{5}$ b) $\frac{1}{3}$ c) $\frac{1}{4}$

Test 28
1. 17
2. 5
3. 51
4. 29
5. 31–35 correct answers
6. 10.00 a.m.
7. 27 km (accept 28 km)
8. 11.20 a.m.
9. 40 km
10. 1 hour 40 minutes

Test 29
Check that the shapes have one extra triangle drawn to make each of them symmetrical.

Test 30

Alternative answers are possible.